The Praise Dance of a Sinner

By Breeze ILifeThis The Poet

American History X/The Praise Dance of a Sinner ©2018 Frederick Eberhardt Jr is Breeze "ILifeThis" The Poet

Editing by: Wendy Jones

Printed in the United States of America 2018

First Edition

Preface

So I'm doing it again. I never really considered myself a much of a writer. I just like words a lot. Enough to respect the power in them. The build and destroy they can accomplish. How a slight switch in tone or context or intention can change a definition, a mind, a feeling, or even a life.

This book is in two parts.

American History X is about another way of looking at issues that surround my culture. Racism and social injustice are often times the result of the media being purposely irresponsible with words. Remember how the bible was used to keep us enslaved. How the slight switch in tone or context or intention can...you get the point.

The Praise Dance of a Sinner is another way of looking at myself. That's really it. Sometimes I'm looking for exits. Sometimes I'm just looking to exist. Sometimes the image is muddied and I can't really make out which one of them is happening. Sometimes I'm weak so I go looking for the power in the words.

Anyway, enjoy it please!!

Sincerely,

Breeze ILifeThis The Poet

Frederick S Eberhardt Jr

Thank You

Wendy,

We did it again!! Thank you so much for believing in me continously!!

My Kids-

Everything I touch is to make you proud of your father!!

Davelyn Hill

My kindred heart

You came into my life and refused to leave

Thank you for that

Iman Briann Boykin, My Water

Thank you for washing love and support over me

You are truly a blessing to a once parched heart

To anyone and everyone that rock with me, listens to me, has inspired me or gives me the honor of inspiring them

You're dope as fuck!!

Thank You

Contents

I-AMERICAN HISTORY X

THE MISEDUCATION OF BLACK SUPREMACY

THE MISEDUCATION OF GIL SCOTT HERON

THE MISEDUCATION OF SAM COOKE

THE MISEDUCATION OF BLACK HISTORY MONTH

THE MISEDUCATION OF TWERKING

THE MISEDUCATION OF TIANA PARKER

MARISSA EXPLAIN IT ALL

II-Intermission

1: In response

2: Lost In Translation

3: A Song For The Ocean

4: Haiku

III-The Praise Dance of a Sinner

1: Fuck Fear

How to be Eaten By a Shark

2: Facebook Salvation

An Open Letter

Split: A Love Story

Unfinished

3: Baptism By Fire

Rules: How to Fall in Love

Untitled

Pt 4: Affirmation

THE MISEDUCATION OF

AMERIKKKAN

HISTORY X

: THE MISEDUCATION OF BLACK SUPREMACY

To the white woman on twitter who said-

Quote: "This is just another example of black supremacy"-

As I wrote this poem I noticed that my black pen doesn't trust this paper anymore-Wonders if the white of this canvas will use its privilege to reword this pens spilled blo-

Ink-

Like most things white tend to do these days-

We are all just super excited to know….

What in the fresh lily white foolishness fuck did you mean….

By…. Black ….Supremacy-

Unless you mean my Grandma sweet potato pie

Must be my auntie fried chicken

The love and genius created in a black mama kitchen

Must be in black women prayer closet how anywhere their knees touch seems to ascend

Black Supremacy must be ascension, how still we rise even under the weight of so much hate, how we climbed out of a 400 plus year grave and still be so live

Black Supremacy must be how we magician, all that black magic, conjuring up some way out of no way, how Baby Dee sell weed, do hair, and babysit all out the same house...they still don't know where to kick the door in at

Must be how pig feet and chitterlings can sound so much like two fish and five loaves

How Harlem made a whole renaissance out of being unheard

Black Supremacy is how we stay winning

A Viola Davis Taraji Henson group piece

Serena being queen enough to serve while crowning a princess

Michael Bennett black fist raise after tackling a white quarterback on the field, is how that sounds like a slave revolt to me

Colin Kaepernick ascending on the sidelines like black women in prayer closets taught him

Issa Rae of pride shining all brilliant at the Emmys like "Im rooting for everybody black, I AM"

Black Supremacy, you must mean, as opposed….to white supremacy

Because it isn't church shootings or church bombings, it's not taking God from us after we found the reflection of its existence in ourselves, when y'all shackled us to the weapon that is religion in the first place

Black Supremacy is not loving your culture means mine is inferior…while stealing and appropriating everything in my so called inferior culture

It's not a hate group…not Neo Nazi…skinhead…KKK hood covering up cops

Politicians

Lawyers

Judges

Black supremacy is a love group

Its Diamond Reynolds patience and strength watching Philando die in front her and her child's eyes

It's the intuition of Korryn Gaines 5yr old knowing those cops we're trying to kill them

Black Supremacy must be embedded in our forgiveness-

Because you're simple ass is still here-

Making dumb ass twitter comments about this stupid shit-

Because we ain't went to war yet-

Come knocking down your damn door yet-

We still ain't burned this bitch down-

So come again...what exactly in the whole heap of white privilege hell is black supremacy again?

Oh...I thought that's what the fuck you meant

: THE MISEDUCATION OF GIL SCOTT HERON

(After Revolution by Jahbu Ourinde)

Hosted by Tomi Lahren-Rachel Dolezal

And starring some of your favorite D list celebrities like

Stacey Dash Raven Symone and Charles Barkley

Live on fox news

The Revolution

The revolution will be posted on Facebook-Followed on Twitter-Snapchatted and instagrammed for the convenience of all too like, comment, gif, jiff...Whatever...Meme, hashtag and poke

Yes ladies and gentlemen people still poking

Video courtesy of WorldStarHipHop-And sponsored by Jordan the official shoe of all riots and marches of the oppressed

Excuse Me...This revolution will have artists artistically and hotepidly illuminating the erectile deficiencies and social atrocities of our struggle by breaking down the complexities of being conscious contradictions

Yeah, you like that, I've been working on my woke

And since the revolution will not be happening at your front door, but from behind the computer screen, please send all donations via Kickstarter to FuckARealRevolution.blah

Speaking of kick starting, the revolution will kicked off with a free concert featuring conscious artists-Such as Lil Such N Such Big whoever and Young What's His Name

This revolution will include all of your favorite appropriators-Excuse me, performers-Such as Justin Timberlake, Iggy Azalea, and Miley Cyrus

And everyone gets a can of new peaceful protest Pepsi

Autographed by Kendall Jenner

This revolution will be on fleek, this revolution gonna be lit, this revolution will even...hit them...folks

As we march to chants like...

"We are not our ancestors... we will fuck you up"

See this revolution will make no mention of Nat Turner,

The St Johns Insurrection

Or The Baptist War

Because this revolution won't know enough about where it's from, to see that we've been here before,

To know where it's going,

Or where to go,

Or how to get there

This revolution will be so delusional in its anger it won't realize that it's mostly only fighting against its own progression

So...yeah... this revolution will be televised

Will be city sanctioned,

Or this revolution will have to ask mama oppressor can it play outside today-Will have a curfew-Will be in before the police lights come on

This revolution will encourage all riots orchestrated by the oppressed-As long as it stays on their side of the street

So this revolution will be overseen by the same cops it's protesting-As they come to serve and protect...Or break your neck...Or illegally choke you out... Or shoot you with your hands up

This revolution believes that the oppressed could simply ask for their freedom from oppressors-Hashtag #Alternative Fact

This revolution will be whitewashed and black faced...Will be full of black stars spewing white noise who don't already know they are dead... Who don't realize revolution also means... Going around in a fucking circle...Right back to into the oppression we were fighting against in the first place

It'll post cute things on Facebook for likes but won't attend the march-It'll camera phone film you getting beat but won't throw a punch

This revolution doesn't need your consent or participation or action

It wants your all black profile pics protests and house arrested outrage-Your half ass black Friday boycotts just to splurge cyber Monday

This revolution wants black women to blame everything on the black men...or black men to blame everything on black women...

This revolution is equal opportunity fucking US over

Guilt free...hassle free...problem free...As long as we never actually...

Get...Free...

This revolution was filmed in front a black lives matter studio audience who watched season after season of this revolution-And died.........laughing

So stay tuned, because this revolution just needs you...to sit there...and keep doing... what you're doing... right......now?

: THE MISEDUCATION OF SAM COOKE

And we heard Sam Cooke sing...

It's been a long, long time coming-

But I know, a change gonna come-

Oh yes it is-

We were told...a change would come...

And despite what we see surface wise with untrained eyes...

They didn't lie...

The changes...as subtle as deception-as deadly as the details-

From salvation to shackle

Slavery to prison

Foreclosed and for sale signs branded in the front the house ya grandpa built with his bare hands sit as righteous as burning crosses when gentrification crashes through windows like Molotov cocktails

Any tool is a weapon depending on how you use it

Like rhetoric that turns murder into mistake and nigger into thug who was asking for it

And we swore this shit wouldn't be televised

Now we just watch...

Yesteryears news...

A nigger reached ascension by way of rope and wrath...

Trying to escape the hell they were told owned their soul-

Caught running towards the pearly gates of freedom

In more recent news…

A Negro child's body was found floating

Washed up on a sure that it will make home today…

At the hands of God fearing fallen angel with Jim Crow wings…

His crime…being charismatic where he don't belong…

Yesterday's news…

An African American…

An alive person of color…

A breathing black body….

Because that is how you say nigger…In today's news

While playing with a toy…

Riding in an ambulance…

Running

In a Walmart…

Selling cds in New York,

Dayton

Charleston

Baltimore

Cleveland

Was escorted off the premises of existing…by a God complex who seen glory in rebuking the sin that is black skin back to Holy Ghost…

A long time coming…but I know

You see the changes…

White sheets beating bodies...black and blue...Turn dress blues covering...black bodies in white sheets

Isn't that a juxtaposition to die for?

Isn't that revisionist history?

Isn't that overseer become officer?

The changes

The tact of attack-The cracking whip-The silence of rope-The splitting of tree branch supporting the dead weight...

Has now become

The opening of wood caskets holding the dead weight-The choke hold splitting oxygen from lungs-The silence of justice-The bang of a gun...the banging of guns...the clip drop...the reload...the bangs from guns...

The changes

In ourselves-Such a recessive nature-Killed our way out of bondage just to die over a trap-Ran towards the hope of future freedom just to march because we mad for a moment we'll forget about in a few days-From revolt to riot to rally to all black social media pics-From behaving like we mattered to now needing a hashtag to remind us

You said a change was gonna come...and a change came Sam-But ain't nobody tell us the difference would be all the same Sam-We have nowhere else to run-And we may not know what's up there beyond the sky-But if it's this hard living, what's the point of being afraid to die

: THE MISEDUCATION OF BLACK HISTORY MONTH

When white people want to know why there is a need for a black history month

I no longer get upset...I've actually allowed myself to entertain this concern...And I must say...I think I understand...

Your issue with being excluded-See when the world usually revolves around you, it may be hard to imagine why anyone else would think their OWN SPACE is beautiful

You must be tired, scrubbing our blood off of your roots is probably a tedious exercise-When white washing can usually clean your prints off of anything

I consider it being hard to swallow without causing cottonmouth-How you would have to have the digestive system of the middle passage to gulp down a genocide without burping up bones

You starving souls, are just desperate for us to understand their diet, how it doesn't go down well with their white wines

So you only chew through us in small, bland, unseasoned appropriation rations

Dr. King speeches and sit-ins-Rosa Parks and peaceful protests-These well done versions cook out the flavor in the meat...because the rare truth be too bloody for you-And you didn't order that type of ugly with your innocence-

The taste of Gabriel's Conspiracy smothered in the Stono Rebellion and served on a bed of Nat Turner revolt is to spicy for you-

Probably burns June 1st, 1921, Black Wall Street going down doesn't it?

When your heritage tried to chef up the enslavement of an entire race-I bet a month of force feeding you our triumphs despite you unsettles your stomach-Bet it smells like chitlins and failure, Jim Crow fried hard with a large helping of we shall overcome sticking to your ribs like soul food-

 But I understand

It's all math for you

And when you only use half a brain to factor in a race you only considered 3/5s a person... the impact of Dr. Charles Drew, Lewis Lattimore, Dr. Patricia Bath, and Sarah Goode becomes an improper fraction you

I get it

The agony of trying to pick the prettiest parts of our history from between your teeth-The exhaustion of carrying the kind or privilege that allows you to ask why we need a black history month and not ask why we need a Columbus Day

Dear White people, I'm here for you

I have collected a palms full of white tears and drank

And i get how February could feel like October to you-How Halloween isn't as fun when the ghost stories aren't fictitious-It feels like a month long trial, and your privilege can't testify away the guilt in your veins when you come from a bloodline of murder weapons

 Yeah, it's hard being white, in America, especially in February-

I'm sorry that anything exist to make things more difficult for YOU than they already are

: THE MISEDUCATION OF TWERKING

There was a time and place when our movement meant something-

Where our walk was royal, our stand was warrior, our being was God-

Until the powers that be translated our truth to better fit their narratives-

Here our royalty sounds like slave, our stand like shackled, our being became based on their perception-

Being field nicca, being house nicca, being property-

Now watch the hands-The smoke, the mirrors-

Notice how being doesn't mean being-

The difference between human being and being human-

See they renamed our narrative into history-

But our movement meant something before we let them define us-

And, now we let them define us-

Now, they just make us forget what we mean here-Memory dissemble here-So whenever you try to remember here-You only remember here-

Example, African dance played an important part in our culture-More than mere entertainment, these dances were rituals for celebrations, reciting history, and interacting with God-

But they make us forget what we mean here-

So they don't call it dancing here-

They call it twerking here, call it ass clapping and pussy popping on a handstand-

The plan...scratch out our sacred till we be the new millennium ManTan-

How he danced to until they black faced and bamboozled his shoe-

They make us forget here what they did to our being-

Watch the hands, the smoke, the mirror-

How capitalism removes culture and now the way we talk to God only made holy in reverence to the root of all evil-And now making it rain, no longer means making it rain-

They make us forget here, what they did to our stand, our walk, our dance-

Wait, no, you can't call it that here-Not dancing here-Not African tradition-Not by its name-

Not Assiko, Adowa, Gombey here-Not Ashanti, Bantu, Yoruba here-Not ancestral, sacred, or free-

That sounds too much like what it really means-

And we need you to forget here, how you got here, that you are not here, remove your meaning so that you only know here-

And here you are-

Where we call it Miley here, JLo here, over sexualize a young black girl's transition into womanhood here-

And now she aint a woman human being here, she a product being sexy here-

You see it, the smoke, the mirror-

How praise dance is snatched from pop lock and drop it....like black women can't do both

And now here you are-

In this new world where they hate what they don't understand and fear what they can't conquer then conjure up ways for us to conquer ourselves-

Example-

Tell them sex sells, so bounce it for a buck, bust it open for a real nigger black queen-

Wait no don't call her that, don't call her queen-Call her miss fat booty hashtag twerk team-Pump her ass with a dose of that baddest bitch syndrome-Till all she knows is how to shake it like a red nose-

You see it-

The smoke, the mirrors-

Because there was a time when our movement meant something-And while they colonize our customs for coins and counterfeit our culture it seems-No one stopped long enough to notice that they never told us what the fuck twerking even means-

: THE MISEDUCATION OF TIANA PARKER

For 7 year old Tiana Parker, who was removed from Deborah Brown Community School due to new rules banning her natural hair style of locks, as well as all other natural hair styles

The principal of Deborah Brown Community School explains

There are guidelines to being a productive figure in today's society-Acceptable attributes that orchestrate the origin of your future importance-Our schools teach kids the tools needed to build success- Things like reading, writing, and arithmetic-When to stand, sit, walk, and run-

Don't speak unless spoken to- stand in line, don't think outside these lines, color in the lines, and keep your color within our lines-

We are teaching kids the essentials to social acceptance-

So when we ask your child's race on standardized test forms, do not question-And when we tell your 7 year old daughter that her hair is not presentable or acceptable-That the royalty evolving in her kinks is "distracting from the serious and respectable atmosphere" the school strives for-When we suggest she trade her afro puffs for pigtails, and her locks for a perm-

Please do not be alarmed black America, this is only a history lesson-Social Studies if you will-The teaching of what being too natural can get you-

That'll get you niggers only employment-

Get you hanging on to a job by a thread around your neck-

Get you slaving for the same cotton your people used to pick-

Did you know that the dollar bill is made up of 75% cotton?-

Oh, the irony-

So, you see why must forget your roots?-

The roots of your hair, the roots of that skin, that root taken to freedom-

You know it ain't free-

Cost Toby a foot-Cost Martin a dream-So what's it worth to you-

How about the kink in your curl for a quarter-

The black power fist at the end of pick for a penny-

Don't get auctioned blocked out of a career-

You will always be nickel and diming unless you shucking and jiving-You know what dancing that jig will get you-

It'll get you fresh white blouse field nigger status-

It'll Sambo smile your Nat Turner-

It'll Barbie your Orisha-

That'll Iggy Azalea your Assata-

Better straight perm and bleach your moonwalker-

Don't make us Lauryn Hill you-

We are Deborah Brown Community School in Tulsa Oklahoma-We are Horizon Science Academy in Ohio-We are the foundation for the building blocks of success-Teaching your kids that in this journey toward the American dream words like culture and natural don't survive-

They won't learn anything from knowing themselves-Success and social acceptance won't understand things like the heritage in their hair-

But if you parents leave it to us, they won't either-

We are gentrifying this great nation of ours-Forcing....excuse me, encouraging you to be better than yourself-Before you have the chance to learn how beautiful you are-Opening the doors to a better tomorrow-Picking one dreaded lock at a time-

You, my dear black America-

Are welcomed/////

MARISSA EXPLAINS IT ALL

Marissa Alexander is a 31 yr. old mother from Florida...who though now recently acquitted...was charged with attempted murder and sentenced to 20 years in prison...for firing a warning shot into the ceiling to protect herself from an abusive husband

This is a letter to my daughter from Marissa Alexander,

Dear Rai'mah Serenity,

We were created as instruments of completion-In my opinion...the purpose of our role is to turn half in to whole-But these days men see more God in us than they can remember being blessed with themselves-So they rule with wrath to convince us we are not to be prayed to, but preyed on-Please do not worship the idol ego of statue like souls-And since they will come for you, this is how you will survive-

Guard your spirit-

Beware of falling promises for by the time they are broken it'll be a black eye to late-Be equipped with the stealthiest of self-esteem-An assassin like silence-You see, its hunting season on anything not labeled broken-

Do not be broken-

They want you as trophy ornament on their war hall walls-And too many of us have found it so easy to play dead-That sometimes we don't have the option of getting up when the game is over-

Understand it's not just Florida-They are everywhere-Cowards that turn predator when they think you don't have the option to fight-Who think that this "stand your ground" shit just makes the prey sexier in their teeth-

Do not be prey-

Be praying-

"Lord forgive him, for he knows not what I'LL do"

Be the twinkle in your Grandmas black eye when your granddad sent a wrecking ball through the widows to her soul-

Be a Tina Turner solo-Be a brass knuckle kiss-Be the woman that doesn't die in this horror movie of a society-

Don't be prey-Don't be a statistic-Don't let them label you survivor like your they one with the sickness-

Be different...be that 38 type special-

Be that woman that a man will never put his hands on-And if a man will put his hands on you-Avenge those we lost in the war on women-

And learn from my mistakes-

Hold yourself steady, intently, like you are created of completion and you intend to stay that way-Rule with the wrath they forgot you were created with-

Do not be broken-

Do not be prey-

Do not be statistic-

And for God's sake-Whatever you do-

DO NOT SHOOT AT THE DAMN CEILING//////

Intermission

Request Granted

"Can you tell me that you would hug me right now if you were near? People say you need a certain number of hugs a day for survival, and I've been operating at an ever increasing deficit for about 8 months"

You have to know that they are scared-

And your love is not prey like how they hunt it, not play dead, not conquest ornament hung from walls-

You are not the teddy bear that they are too childish to cherish-That'll get lost or replaced with the next new toy they are ready to destroy-

They stay far away because their intentions wouldn't survive such an encounter-They know your love can smell fear-And it's not supposed to be here-The live and uncaged of your love in a natural habitat would be too much beauty for feeble eyes-

You are not exhibit showcase or domesticated, not for the consumption of bear trap embrace-

You have the heart of a grizzly-It takes a special kind of people to not get crushed in the force of your passion-

So this is for you, to know that my chest will always be a forest you can roar in as loud and fierce as you need to-A cave for your soul to hibernate in-

I will be there for you to pour all of your too much into-I am not afraid of your strength-Will not attack you when you are down or cower at how big you are when standing on your love-

It's a jungle out there, and a love like yours has a lot of known enemies-But if you ever need to use my arms as refuge-My shoulders safe haven from predatory promises-Just know, the answer is always yes, I will always, most definitely hug you

Lost In Translation

The taste of intent dying on our tongue

The sound of her fleeing footsteps clawing the ground to get back to me

The hole i put in the wall crooning with passion

The moment after she left echoing off the clock to loud for me to sleep

It's only been 30 minutes

But-I miss her

But she can't know that

See we burn the prints off of our words like we can't leave any evidence that we actually care

But we tear the hinges off of trust with search warrants looking for ulterior motives

Swallow the sound of understanding and regurgitate already resolved issues

Tell each other to leave when we really don't want to be alone

And we never consider where our hearts go when we send it out of the room because grown folks talking

Using elementary responses and playground bully tactics

I'll call you stupid but hope you know i think your smile is brilliant-You'll toss my sincerity in the trash like finger paint portraits and macaroni necklaces-When you really think it's beautiful enough to be hung on the fridge

I'll provoke you to be noticed -You'll ignore me to get my attention-Till we are both fighting just to feel each other

We get so lost in translation

Let the past hug our lungs like cigarette smoke till we croak out cancerous notions when we really just want to be able to breathe each other

Lose our voice and press insecurities into our throats like an electrolarynx

And forget to realize that we didn't always used to sound like this

Back before we weren't too cool to feel

Before it wasn't so important to be cool

Now we can't take this so called cool off long enough to save ourselves from frostbitten feelings

Look I don't want to argue-

This is not what I meant-

I meant I'm hurting, just come heal me

I meant to say that subject is touchy so please try to feel me

I meant I wish you would come back

I meant I Love You

But this misleading language got us lost in translation and I don't want to be here anymore

I been driving myself crazy and talking in circles trying to say the right things to get back to you heart

I've been told its where home is

A Song for the Ocean

When you asked if I'm in love

I bet Lenny cried listening to the song Donny was singing for you

Stevie could see the purple reign imperially in your heart

I could hear him telling you it's the color of royalty

But Prince said this is America, they are scared of beautiful here

There will be tears

Is that what took you so long

Was hate crime lodged in your throat?

Did it taste like Matthew Shepard's name in your mouth?

Was the thought Thapelo Makhutle like nova cane when it hurt too much speak his name?

Were you so scared to think about your forever?

Because they don't think that far ahead here

See here they practice the bad religion of social acceptance

Pour judgment like cyanide in Styrofoam cups

It's either drink or kill yourself trying to hold on to a disguise

Either way it's suicide

Is this why you figured you couldn't get God to love you

I've been wondering what made you admit it

Were you watching yourself sing "I miss you" live, seen his face in your lyrics and realize you couldn't hide from apart of yourself so easily?

Did you get paranoid and confess thinking everyone would find out anyway?

Because love has a tendency to glow through the cracks when hidden

And yours had a pinkish aura surrounding you on that stage

Is that his favorite color?

Did it make you want to shed the pseudo perception of an image and go tell it on a stage?

Or in an interview

Or a mountain that his existence made you matter

That that Pink matters

Did you finally get it?

That it don't matter who you are, it's so simple, a feeling

But it's everything

And it don't matter who you love, it's so simple, a feeling

But it's everything

That love is EVERYTHING

Not the bewilderment of pond minded people behind all the dam of wondering how he could flow like water into your spirit

Sexuality is fluid and you are an ocean

You have no boundaries

Frank I don't mean to pry into the bible bleeding out of your scars but i have been meaning to talk to God more

And that love you have is the closest thing to scripture i can comprehend without man made gavels banging my desires into a guilty conscious

I just want to say thank you for embracing what natural feels

For diving head first into whatever makes you float

I want you to enjoy it

Kick off those shoes

Take off that suit

And swim good

Haiku

Gentrified love is

You tear me down to build a

Me I can't afford

                If a heart is a

            House of love, then her heart is

              Section eight housing

                                  I jumped into love

                            She caught me, like a cliff edge

                                  Catches a trust fall

              Just because you got

            In her ribs, doesn't mean you're

              Closer to her heart

Rebuke the gospel

Of split tongue sermons the

Devil knows scripture too

              Dear Penis, love does

              Not need any help, you are

              Just fucking things up

                                I can't trust your words

                            If actions aren't as consistent

                                  As my demons

The Praise Dance
of a Sinner

Pt. 1-Fuck Fear

This poem is a prayer-

Rebuking, removing, and defeating the spirit of fear from your life

This poem has many names but does not have a title, this poem is a working title if you listen closely you'll realize the work is in the title

So this poem is called

When the brilliant black boy writes battle bars for Satan

Or

When the gorgeous black girl realizes she is God therefore prayers to her reflection when religion aint enough

Or

When the genius black child considers praying in native tongue cause if God is up there listening

So this poem is called

Although I walk through the valley of the shadow of death, I shall fear no evil

The genius, brilliant, gorgeous black child remix

So, this poem is called

I guess I got my swagger back, the devil tried to kill me y'all but I guess I got the dagger back

Or

The gospel according to Bone Crusher-Bitch I ain't ever scared

Or

How to use Kirk Franklin Hello Fear album as an oxygen mask in the gas chamber of give up

Or

How to use an ultra-light beam as a night light to finish your coloring book while eating Sunday Candy in the dark of doubt

No, this poem is called

A heart is a house of love

Or

Love and Fear can't exist in the same space

Or

When the heart serves Fear its eviction notice-

No, this poem is called

I almost gave up today

Subtitle: but my daughters smile

Or

But my sons laugh

Or

But my mamas prayers

Or

But Nah!!

But Can't Stop Won't Stop!!

But I'm Good Love, Enjoy!!

No, this poem is called

Faith never left, it just plays hide and seek at the worst times, which is always the perfect time, hides in the places you always forget to look first, like the last place you saw God

Or

This poem is called

The praise dance of a sinner: A Fight Song for the scared to start over-because sometimes your Genesis gets engulfed in darkness when circumstances make you forget how to speak yourself a light-

 No, this poem is called

That one time Fear was talking shit like-

Poem:

I better not catch you walking through the valley of the shadow of death, I be the darkness there, heavy in them streets, so heavy you won't be able to lift your voice-you think you bad huh, try me then, and see if I don't choke the let there be right out of you

Or

This poem is called

The Pull Up: Cause the devil be talking shit

Poem:

Yeah I walk through the valley of the shadow of death often- and Bitch I ain't ever scared-I got my swagger back- you tried to kill me but I'm up in you spot looking like Sunday Candy-An ultra-light beam awesome in all that nothing-Yeah I found faith, it never left, it was just playing hide and seek with the prayers laughs and smiles, coloring book bright and hiding in the last place I saw God-So tell me again, what's all that dark about when I am the light he let there be

No, this poem is called

A Sundays Worst for your Wednesday Praise and Worship

Or

How I talk to God, cause he already know my lil ratchet ass heart understands the difference between cursing someone and cursing a hoe ass devil out in the joyful noise

No, this poem is called

"Cussing in church"-the testimony of a heathen that God ain't through with...as long as I ain't through with myself

This poem is called

Every breath I take is a middle finger praise dancing to the drum of "I almost gave up today....

But Nah-

I'm Good Love, Enjoy"

So this poem is called

The brilliant gorgeous ghetto child writes a diss track for the devil-

Poem:

Hello Fear, Fuck You!! And Amen!!

How to be Eaten

So the psychiatrist says…"Frederick, there is an animal in all of us that relates with how we function…how we think…how we survive. A spirit animal if you will. Knowing your animal is an understanding of self how you will thrive…fight…and eventually even be destroyed"

 How to be eaten by a shark-

Swim away-

Fast-

There is failure in your current-

You are not floating, you are sinking-

You have to move-

Retreat-

Think about all the lives that depend on your survival-

Leave them for dead-

It'll save they're life to not carry the weight of them-

Don't imagine they would be just as happy being devoured in your arms-

Just focus on your suffocating embrace and GO!!-

Chase life like you do for a living-

Move-

Richmond-

Virginia Beach-

Greenville-

Charlotte-

Flee from all the unsure of life into the carnivorous teeth of certainty-

Splash around and make yourself seen-

And he will chase you like a blessing-

Remember, that's all you've ever wanted to be

A blessing-

Needed-

Look where that got you-

Staring down the mouth of a prayer looking like an answer-

Thank God for understanding-

Notice its stride-

You can tell it has children-

Nothing else to rely on-

You've seen this hunger before-

It looks like girlfriends that last longer than three months-

It looks like bus tickets and money order receipts-

It looks like back child support and birthdays-

It looks like 34 with nothing to show for it-

It looks like if it stops moving it'll die-

Won't you?-

Do not shy away from your purpose-

Own it-

You've spent your entire story editing yourself-

You deserve to catch every moment of the end-

There will be thoughts of better ways to do this-

Forget them, sometimes wrong is how it was supposed to be-

It won't be hard-

Wrong is how it's always been-

Ex-wife, step dad, the military, depression-

Wrong is the perfect seasoning to such a meal-

Look at its grin-

Snarled back lips will reveal a pitchfork filled teeth-

You will remember smiles with similar intentions-

All the demons you fought-

At least you know this one is genuine-

This will be quick-

Not like your relationships-

Or your circumstances-

Or your piranha like perception constantly tearing yourself apart-

It is not trying to kill you-

It's just tired, has been moving all day, trying not to die, all while starving to death-

You know this cycle, you know this hunger-

So don't demean this into a mistake

Overthink this into a suicide-

Or debate this into something other than God's plan-

You understand this-

As confused as you have been about the way things are-

And where you belong-

Haven't you found a home here-?

You have always been in the business of giving of yourself-

Tearing yourself limb from limb to find your holy-

Confined to your own consumption to be something beautiful-

And here you are-

Looking like a whole snack-

Embrace the blessing-

This...makes it all make sense/////

Pt. 2-Facebook Salvation

Depression is mute button...lodged in my throat...that is pressed whenever any kind of logic about how I'm feeling gets loud enough for anyone to actually hear...

Which then results in people misunderstanding almost everything I say...which in fact makes depression even more the silent killer it's always been

When this happens...I pray to the holy Marc Zuckerberg for a voice...and he answers in question form like some sort of parable...

"What's on your mind"?

And isn't that like a mean God...that sees you struggling to stand on faith but still makes you walk to your own salvation...

Anyway...

I begin to release post after post about this finger trap brain that won't let me let go of these thoughts...Won't let me out regardless of how much I push in...When I try to pull out of my depression it just gets tighter...

I do this...and loved ones tell me to stop...say I need to go to the confession booth instead...which is to say I need a therapist...say I practice a bad religion in telling all my business to people who don't care...and I think...

"But aren't you here too?"

One time a friend told me the way I talk about myself is disgusting to her...makes her wonder how I talk about her behind her back...

I was unaware of how my way out would be a finger trap to others...until she showed me her hands stuck in how disgusted I make her...

And now I don't post on Facebook much because I know she'll see it...and I haven't heard from her since...

And isn't that like a mean God...to take away all you have and expect the empty to fill you...

And now I don't know who to pray to anymore...

I pray to God and the silence is depressing...

I pray to depression to stop being such a mean God...and He scolds me like he did Job for asking questions

I pray to Facebook and the congregation gets uncomfortable...which is depressing...

I would pray to myself...but I already tried praying to depression...and I couldn't make any sense of what or how I was feeling...

And there goes that finger trap again...holding me hostage...and yes I'm on my knees...but it's different when you're at gunpoint...

When you're holding the gun...

These days...I don't post about it on Facebook much...I sit alone and study the scripture that is depression poems from the bible of YouTube...book of Button...

When I see others post about their depression...

I leave a like...because I like the fact that they are trying to push in...And I'm ok with how they release...

I leave a heart...so hopefully they know that when theirs hurts...they can share mine...

I leave a comment...so hopefully they know we can talk...

I don't leave a sad face...because I won't make their prayer about my sadness...because depression is a jealous mean God...and I don't want to look like wrath to them...

And I don't

Under any circumstances say

Pray about it.....

Sheets Speak... An Open Letter

Quote-"I wonder what my bed sheets say about me when I'm not around"-Rudy Francisco

An open letter from the bed sheets of Frederick Eberhardt Jr.

He climbs into me, hesitantly

Confident in my love for him-

Trusting that I will always hold him like no one else will

But I am a painful reminder

That no one else will

The road to his hell is paved with my good intentions

He's been looking for love for so long

Promises his reflection that he won't rest until he has it

And he returns to me empty hearted

Tired and defeated and my skin must be a waving flag shade of white

I must be salt in his wounded wishes

The light at the end of a tunnel that his faith was last seen fleeting towards

As I entice his weary body to relax

Seduce him to break his promise to a reflection that didn't believe him in the first place

He crashes into me, a kamikaze, a final stand in a lost war

His body awkward like it's a joke he knows he's the butt of

He never changes me

Thinks he'll ruin me in the wash

Knows washing don't work

Lonely don't wash out

The walls be talking

Said they overheard the pillowcases complaining about the weight of his nightmares

The wash clothes say he scrubs so hard but his skin still feels the filth of untouched after showers

He's the laughing stock of the linen closet

His dreams bully him

Make him believe that love still exists

Taunt him about how his resting is the reason he can't find it

So some nights he doesn't rest

Goes looking for forever

Making wishing wells out of women like maybe if his prayers can reach the bottom of their deep they'll come true for him

So he bring these lies home and lies them into my pureness

Unholy hallelujahs and sacrificial sweat stain my holy,

Pierce my skin like stigmata marks

Then they leave

And the stench of abandonment chisels itself into me

I feel like this is all my fault-

Like my prayers reach God's ears before his do

I just want him to rest

But i can't really verbalize how i feel

So I just lay here and write him love poems with the ink of his tears

Tuck my secrets between the mattress of this king size diary

Hide smirks as he lies to his reflection every morning

Feel a sense of satisfaction when he returns

Wrap my edges around him and rub my softness into his skin

I desire what he fears most

The nights he leaks into my band aid embrace a fresh cut failure are when I find the love he's been searching for

Dear Rudy Francisco

I am replying to a poem you wrote that I overheard him listening to the other day, contrary to popular opinion the walls talking are the least of your worries, but when the sheets speak, you may not be ready to lay comfortably in this kind of truth

And with that, I implore you

Don't ask questions that you don't want the answers to

Split: A Love Story

Hey, I have a question, what's the difference between Frederick and Breeze?

Wow, that's a good one-

I never really considered there being a differ......

Well, I would answer you- but first I'd have to know who you're asking?- Or wait I have a question, what's difference between a therapist and some nosey person screwing with my head-cause you know you're not a therapist right- So that would make you a nosey person, just screw...

Fred always gets like this-Protects everything he wants to give people, from people-He's like a guard dog that really would love to play fetch-but he refuses to let go of the stick, or the ball, or his heart, or his demons-He want you to see him-He just doesn't want to be exposed-He's very abstract art-paints passion into how he loves-but can only picture the pain and broken that loving hard has left him-so all you end up with is a beautifully shattered, open wound of a heart on the canvas of his tongue

I don't know how to explain, but kind of reminds me of that one movie,

Okay, you know what, let's talk about Breeze The Poet-The lover-who puts it in his art-Writes to love himself free-and sharing this freedom is how he gives his love-But that's so stupid- He's not free just because he can cleverly articulate his chains-It's funny when he takes his shoes off on stage- As if the space is safe for him, but there is nothing safe about bleeding pretty for people who aren't going to help him clean up the mess he makes of himself- chant go in poet-and never even consider how the fuck he'll get out----

I get it though, why he's so guarded-He hates being misunderstood and people don't even try-It's just easier to sit comfortable in their assumptions-and use him as a scapegoat to justify how badly they treat him-I see how he's been caution taped into a cage-And now he's a crime scene-I wish he'd stop carrying himself like a suicide weapon-killing off the best part of...

The movie where the guy kidnaps a few girls, and has a bunch of personalities trying to control his body, I think they call him The Hoard

Oh wait I get it now, you're using Breeze's openness to expose my how closed I am, but this open space has only made him a gun range, a bulls eye-a target for rifle rhetoric-he doesn't get it, love is a fighting word- that's why the heart is the size of a fist in the fucking first place-he's so weak- fair game trying love the bang off of a bullet, willing to slow dance with shotgun mouths just to be a trophy on a wall-

I'm tired of him calling me weak, he doesn't know it takes power to hold on to something-He lives in fear, really just a coward who measures his strength on how far he can push people away-

Breeze is a buffet of trauma offering himself up for everyone to pick through his scars-They get full off his faults and leave without finishing their plates-Till all that's left are tables dirtied with the scraps of him they leave behind-

They always leave us behind---

Split yeah, that's the name of the po...excuse me, the movie-It's called Split-

Anyway I don't know how to answer your question, all I can tell you, is if there is a difference-

I hope it's possible to-

Just Love/*Just Love*

All of...Me

Unfinished

To be or not to be...

That is the turmoil that troubles my existence-

To be black...

To be straight...

To be male

Is to be the problem by default

Being labeled cist het like a slur

To be the new nigger with the hard er

To be the enemy of a people I will fall on my own sword to protect

To be victim and villain

To be victim...until I voice that I'm attacked..."well now you're just playing victim"

To be trash in their eyes no matter how much I treasure them

To be villain...whether I'm the bad guy or not...

If I don't accept villain...and won't allow myself to be victim...

Then all I'm left with

 Is not to be

 When I was 30 I was raped...

Woke up in a car to a woman who didn't even have the courtesy to even seem like she assumed I wanted this...ravaging through me like a vulture does an already dead thing

Because already dead things don't get a choice in what happens to their carcass

I said no...I don't want to...repeatedly...pushed back with her on top of me while the seatbelt held me down like an accomplice...fought back...as much as a black male can be victim without becoming villain

Because there's a fine line between rape and domestic abuse

Not to be a victim or to be a bitch for hitting a woman

Because these hands can make love and war but no one tells us what to do when women literally use sex as a weapon

I gave up...gave in...Confused...conceded fucked back with all the anger and energy i wasn't allowed to use to protect myself...like a man should,

I guess

She came...

I didn't...

I got out the car and walked home crying...

When I recalled this back to her...she cried...and her tears meant more to me than mine...

When I recalled this back to my best friend...a black male, he said...oh um..."yeah...that's rape"...and his awkward meant more to me than mine

When I recalled this to my ex...she said..."wait...how...I'd imagined you would like waking up to sex...I'd think you'd have wanted that"...

What I heard was you're a man...in a car with a woman...sleeping...you asked for it

What I heard was my masculinity questioned...because all real men want that right?

What I didn't hear was her ask me why I didn't want it

What I didn't hear was her care to know the details

When I recalled this back to my ex-

She was confused, and her confusion meant more to me than mine

And this is my view of a black man in America today...

To be awkward...uncomfortable...confused about the right way to be until I ask...but asking means I should have already known

Asking to be debating...to be villain and not to be heard

To be crying...except my masculinity brings my tears into question...be too toxic to touch that subject...in which I am playing victim and not to be considered

Days ago...these same hands that couldn't fight a woman off of me while being raped

Were used to fight a man assaulting a woman on a public sidewalk

I got jumped

The other guy, joined in like a seatbelt

I endured this, because it's the man I am that is not considered

Because to be a man...is to be protector

Even if it's protecting the people who attack me

Is to be aware that though I'm not every man...every man also aint me

Is to not be seen as man, but be included with all men

Responsible for all men

To be understanding of the fact that there are very good reasons why our women don't feel protected by us

And disheartened at how impossible it seems not to be them

Pt 3: Baptism by Fire

The moment my feet touched the tabernacle of your city...

The last place I took part of the communion of your holy...

I felt the ghost of orgasms pasts...

My spirit became amplified at the memory of the joyful noise of your moans...

The thoughts rushed back to the matrimony of our bones...

How you used to sit on this hard wood pew and praise dance problems away...

How I was blessed enough to speak a sermon into the mouth of the body of what had to be the wet Jesus walked on

And I felt alive for you again...

Like purpose...

And now I miss you...to death

I want you to kiss me like a casket kisses a corpse...

A place for the dead of me to rest...

A warm place for all the cold decay inside this chest...

Or maybe I'm bugging....

Lying to myself...

And maybe I just want don't want to call the dead thing by its name...

US...Cause the thought of us is the dead thing...

And my mind is the casket...

And I'm praying for a resurrection...

So I'm back at the sanctuary of your smile...

Like Jesus revisiting the tomb trying to figure out where he left the third day...

Searching for the miracle...

The rise...

And maybe I just wish we could be reborn...

But isn't it funny how undying love could be the yearning for a matrimony of bones even if all you come up with is corpse...

Anyway I'm in your city, and I miss you

Or maybe I'm bugging again...

And just don't want to call convenience what it is...

Would rather call it undying love...like undead...like zombie love...

And isn't whatever is pumping all this sick blood through my veins the problem in the first place...

Like if I gave you my heart...

And it was dead...

You would be purpose...Right?

A place to be alive and warm in...

And isn't that like man...throwing around all his nothing like a prize...giving away his dead to be reborn at the expense of the womb...

You were heaven to me...

And maybe I lost all my reason to feel like a God without you...

Or maybe you are God

Like giver of life and I'm the dead thing...

And I'm back at the tabernacle of your city

Because anywhere you are is sacred ground...

And maybe I need you to move this rock again

Just want to congregate our flesh and sing a scripture into the temple of you

Or maybe this lonely in these dead bones is too much hell to deal with on my own

Either way it's brought me to my knees

Full of shit and sin and seeking salvation in any sanctuary I can find

Trying to find a way out the wilderness of my own lonely

Yeah, maybe you are God, and I'm on my knees, because that's where you come to me most

And I'm just trying to remember how to pray

Rules: How to Fall in Love

With a Married Woman

Caution...please read all warning labels before proceeding-

1. Leave your hat where it is-There is no place for you to lay it here-This whole scene is about the temptations-Not a place of rest-Kick your shoes off and get comfortable in-Don't unpack-Your excess baggage is not welcomed-You are a rolling stone-She is a cliff edge-To venture farther than she is willing to go is to shatter at her feet-So please, do not fall for her-

(N)Otis, ain't nobody coming to see you

2. Always remember that relationships are like suicide....they both take commitment...She will hold on to the idea of you for dear life...support...her...but know that he can pull the plug any time...so decide now if she's worth dying for

3. As you Christopher Columbus your way into her heart-It maybe best that you always remember-That you are GOING THE WRONG FUCKING WAY

4. You may feel the sudden urge to want more-may start to doing weird things-Unscheduled calls-reaching for the empty next to you in your sleep-see things her in places she doesn't belong...like the future-This is quite natural-You are just experiencing feelings-all you need to do is direct yourself to the nearest seat....and have it-

Im mean be serious-You can't possibly trust your feelings-how do you think got you here in the first place-Feeling lonely-Feeling insecure-Feeling desperate enough to think you can find love here, you can't even think about love when you don't love yourself-If you did you wouldn't be making this list poem placing blame and hurt on anyone but yourself-You made the decision to devalue yourself-You put yourself on sale-Discounted for defects to your heart and she was bargain shopping-for a way out of her hell-She didn't do anything you weren't already doing to yourself---------

Excuse me, seems we had some technical difficulties, now where were we, ah yes-

5.   When **CHEATING...**Stop it- When **COMMITTING ADULTERY...** No-When making lo....**hell no not even close, when fuc**....having sex...*snatches mic*

if she ever tells you that she can feel you in her ribs she's probably lying....also, it does not mean that you are any closer to her heart...So do not allow yourself to become comfortable with her sex...You must fuck her like it is the last time every time-fuck hard-give her all of your pain as pleasure so you are not the only masochists in this situationship-

fuck her until she cums so hard...she doesn't leave...again-

Maybe-

But more than likely, she will-

So do not ask her if the pussy is yours-IT IS NOT YOURS-she is lending this to you-You are borrowing this-She will just as quickly evict you from her orgasms to renovate her "walls" for the owner-because you are just leasing this pussy until the mortgage comes home

So Warning-

The one you were supposed to read before proceeding- When falling in love with a married woman-

DON'T!!

Untitled

Please stop asking people who are in volatile situations why they stay,

It's because volatile, means to change rapidly and unpredictably especially for the worst

Especially

Not certainly,

And that taste like faith on the tongue of stubborn passion

I mean wouldn't she see love and want to become it?

And "it's probably going to get worse before it gets better",

Sounds like scripture to me

Sounds like God in so many things

I mean Jonah was swallowed by a whale,

Job endure God's wrath

The prodigal son ate with pigs-

So is this broken heart God's doing?

Was I disobedient?

Or was I just a trump spade to be played in a pissing match with the devil?

Is she God?-

And this is some mystery ministering from atop mountains of madness

Or is she not God?

And I've been doing this all wrong?

Is this a message to stand fast in the wake of Her wrath?

Or is it punishment for the way I worshipped her?

I don't believe in the bible anymore

But I believed in Her like scripture

That she is love

That Her will be done if I prayed to her enough

That if she be so powerful, she can crack the rib she is to me and remove the heart I vowed to her

The assuredly She can fix it back

Or did that idea only exist because I believed in her

And that's why we stay-

Because we've been taught pain and love are synonymous-

That the struggle of having your heartbroken be a trial worth testimony-

An alter call effort to not say an angered god's name in vain

So we pray for patience

Until we are too busy on our knees

To get up

And walk away

Pt 4: Affirmation

Scene...my ex says

"I'm leaving you...but don't move on...just wait for me to get over myself"

A sermon entitled-

The praise dance of a sinner: An affirmation of worthy

Or-

When my ex THOUGHT she could do all things through Christ who strengthens her, didn't read the part where it clearly states EXCEPT COME FOR ME

Or-

Lawd, forgive her for she know not who the fuck she talking to

Consider ye this holy day

The book says, "In all of your getting, get understanding"

But it's such a blessing what can be siphoned out of the not getting-

See, it was in the not getting, that the God in me was rediscovered unto myself amidst the hell I been through

Reminded me that I am created in the image of something greater than what I allowed myself to become

See I was fat from all that empty-

So full of all the nothing I devoured and gave thanks for-

The lack of attention that made me ignore my reflection-

The lazy that made my love feel like hard labor-

The selfish that made my giving unfulfilling-

 I was malnourished from this table scrap love and fast food affection-

But blessed the day I looked in the mirror and saw ribs collards baked macaroni and big mama biscuits-The day I fed myself so much of me that I became too full on my reflection to be her leftovers-

I made her a miracle and still only got a crucifixion to show for it-

Was left for dead and forced to move that boulder off my chest on my own-

But glory, I moved that fucking rock on my own-

And noticed that it wasn't until I filled the holes in my hands with myself that I felt anything like a savior-

 This be the joyful noise I raise to the heavens-

Affirming what I am and rebuking everything I am not-

 I am not your maybe-

Not the giver of my all to your bottomless-

Or worshipper of your dirt when you won't treasure me-

I am not the soil you stand on but never plant yourself into-

I am not barren-

But you can only grow here if you sowed here-

I am not broken-

Not breaking-

I didn't break this, it was broken when I got here-

I just stayed long enough trying to fix us to get blamed for it-

But I am not your guilt-

Here to be blamed for all the crimes committed to your heart-

You will not convict me of killing your faith and sentence me to kinda sorta love-

I will not let you please baby please me into plea bargain-

Take a deal for less than I'm worth because I'm scared of solitary confinement-

I gave you this heart-

Cleaned house of it and made myself into a home for you-

But I am not your chore-

A plot for your procrastination-

I am not your vacation-

An escape-

A beachfront away from your blues, worth more than a timeshare tolerance-

A place you know won't interfere in your life, but will always be there when you get back-

I made you priority-

Made a decision to give you the value of my attention-

You were incapable of doing the same-

And in not getting that from you, I am reminded that I am worth choosing-

Even if I have to choose myself-

And if I can't be the choice

Then what I will get out of all the nothing you had to offer

Is to choose me

And never allow myself

To be anybodies-

Fucking option-

AND AMEN-

AND ONE MORE AMEN///

Breeze "ILifeThis" The Poet, born Frederick S Eberhardt Jr, is a native of Richmond, Virginia. A spoken word artist professionally for 8 years now, the 6 time King of the South Regional Poetry Slam Champion and 2018 National Poetry Slam Champion has done some pretty cool things this early in his career. From performing at the historic Apollo Theater in New York City to being featured on season 4 of the hit television series Lexus presents TV1 Verses and Flow. His first self-published book, Serenity Song: Whole Hymns for Broken Peace, was a big success. And we're certain his 2nd self-published work, American History X: The Miseducation of.../The Praise Dance of a Sinner, is going to be even bigger!!

Made in the USA
Middletown, DE
09 October 2022

12257300R00040